The Hamptons

The Hamptons

Text by

Dianne and Don Judd

Photography by Claudia Parks

CLB 2579
© 1991 Colour Library Books Ltd, Godalming, Surrey, England.
All rights reserved.
This 1991 edition published by Crescent Books,
distributed by Outlet Book Company, Inc, a Random House Company,
225 Park Avenue South, New York, New York 10003.
Color separations by Scantrans Pte Ltd, Singapore.
Printed and bound in Hong Kong.
ISBN 0 517 05311 X
8 7 6 5 4 3 2 1

CRESCENT BOOKS
NEW YORK

Looking sunset-ward from Westhampton, where the Hamptons begin.

Seventy-five miles east of New York City, at Riverhead, the county seat of Suffolk, Long Island splits into two forks divided by Great Peconic Bay. It is the South Fork that we are concerned with here, in particular that string of towns along the fork known collectively as "The Hamptons." This region is almost fifty miles in length but, for convenience, it can be broken into three areas, clustered around the towns of Westhampton, Southampton and East Hampton. Approaching the area from the west, we will first explore the western Hampton area, a fifteen mile stretch of land that encompasses Eastport, Westhampton, Quogue, Hampton Bays and the Shinnecock Canal. The central Hampton region revolves around the two villages of Southampton and Sag Harbor, while the eastern Hamptons begin at Sag Harbor and continue through East Hampton, winding up at the familiar lighthouse at Montauk Point.

The waves rolling in from the Atlantic Ocean exert an endlessly fascinating attraction for visitors to Long Island's South Fork.

Today, the Hamptons are best known as the summer vacation spot of celebrities, socialites, executives, politicians, artists and writers, most of whom are seeking temporary refuge from the hectic pace of New York City. Attracted by the natural beauty and seclusion of the area, vacationers started coming to the Hamptons toward the end of the last century. They came to the South Fork because it is blessed with some of the world's most beautiful ocean beaches along with bays and inlets that are ideal for fishing. During the season – marked at each end by the Memorial and Labor Day weekends – thousands of people from all over the world now come to the Hamptons, creating a lively holiday atmosphere.

All of Long Island was formed during the most recent ice age by the advance and retreat of the glaciers. The glaciers formed two distinct geographical features: the North Fork was created by one glacier while the South Fork, all the way through to Montauk Point, was formed by another, known as the Ronkonkoma Moraine. As the glaciers retreated, they left the Atlantic Ocean to do its work on the heap of stones and fertile rubble left behind. Along the South Fork of Long Island, the Atlantic Ocean built up a series of barrier islands, which formed bays and inlets such as Moriches Bay and Shinnecock Bay. The Atlantic continues its work today, sometimes even breaking through the same barrier islands it once created, as occurred in the hurricane of 1938, when Shinnecock inlet was formed.

This area was first settled more than 4,000 years ago, when tribes of the Algonquin nation found a green and

The long shadows of a fall afternoon stretch over the neatly combed earth of this East Hampton farm.

pleasant land populated with small game and surrounded by bays and ponds chock full of fish and shellfish, all thriving in the mild coastal climate. The Indians lived in harmony with their surroundings until the arrival of European settlers in the seventeenth century. These newcomers, the first wave of whom came from the New England colonies of Connecticut and Massachusetts, quickly spread throughout the South Fork. They purchased and appropriated land from the Indians until all that remains for Native Americans today is the Shinnecock Indian Reservation near Southampton. In the 1700s, one major source of livelihood was the raising of cattle, horses and sheep. It was the ranchers who laid out Montauk Highway (Route 27), the major artery that runs through the Hamptons and the route that we will follow eastward. In the eighteenth and nineteenth centuries, agriculture spread as ranching diminished in importance and the land was turned over to the cultivation of vegetables. The soil and climate were well suited to the growing of potatoes and Long Island soon became identified with this, its most famous crop. In the mid-nineteenth century, a new industry developed along the bays and inlets of the South Fork with the introduction of ducks from China, and soon Long Island duckling was featured on the menus of prominent New York City restaurants. Then, in recent years, it was discovered that this same climate and soil would produce excellent grapes, giving birth to the Long Island wine industry. One of the pleasures of visiting the Hamptons is the opportunity it affords to sample restaurants that serve the

Along with seaweed and seashells, the receding Atlantic leaves tidal pools for all to enjoy.

regional fare – Long Island duckling, potatoes, Peconic Bay scallops, clams, oysters, flounders, and a good Chardonnay from a local vineyard.

The prosperity that these products brought to the area is reflected in the local estates, which are built in a wide range of architectural styles. The seventeenth- and eighteenth-century homes mirror the architectural tradition of New England, and are most often in the saltbox or windmill styles. Sag Harbor and Bridgehampton, in particular, boast examples of nineteenth-century Federal and Greek Revival styles of architecture. But it was not until the late nineteenth and early twentieth centuries that what could be called the Hampton style of residential architecture evolved. This is a variation known as the Shingle Style home, and it is characterized by a wood-framed house, hung with weathered shingles, surrounded by a broad expanse of well-manicured lawn and protected by a thick, carefully tended privet hedge. Since privacy is at a premium in the Hamptons, these hedges often attain heights of twelve to fifteen feet.

Superimposed against this backdrop of traditional homes is a new wave of modern and post-modern houses, which has rapidly spread throughout the area. Along Dune Road in Westhampton, a variety of modern styles stand shoulder to shoulder, all facing the Atlantic Ocean together. The former potato farms of Sagaponack now boast ultra-modern architectural concoctions on their land, while Montauk has witnessed a resurgence in building to accommodate the growing population at the extreme tip of the island. The Hamptons of the late

Broccoli, cabbage and cauliflower compete with traditional Long Island potatoes for the diminishing farmland in East Hampton.

Reading is an outdoor lawn activity in the summer.

twentieth century are growing rapidly as increasing numbers of people seek an escape from New York City. At the same time, preservation and conservation are of major concern here, and the natural beauty of the area is still evident despite its continuing development. Today's visitor to the Hamptons is fortunate in being able to experience the area's history. The Indian heritage lives on not only in the place names of Shinnecock, Montauk, Quogue, and Amagansett, but also in the Shinnecock Indian Reservation, where native crafts, traditions and culture are preserved. The coming of the settlers from New England is commemorated in a monument at

Conscience Point in the town of North Sea. Meanwhile, Walt Whitman, who grew up on Long Island, captured the joy of spending his childhood amidst the natural beauty of the area when he wrote:

"O to have been brought up on bays, lagoons, creeks or along the coast,
To continue and be employ'd there all my life,
The briny and damp smell, the shore, the salt weeds exposed at low water,
The work of fishermen, the work of the eel fisher and clam-fisher."

Right: fourth of July enjoyment in Sag Harbor.

THE WESTERN HAMPTON AREA

We begin our ride along Montauk Highway in Eastport, and as we cross Seatuck Creek, we have entered the boundaries of Southampton Township. A worthwhile detour south from the highway brings us to the area called Remsenburg, which recreates the early-nineteenth-century atmosphere of the Western Hamptons. The main street is lined with large trees and an assortment of charming homes, enclosed by white picket fences. Many of the buildings proudly display the dates of their construction, and several date back to the early 1800s, while the white, shingled Presbyterian Chapel was built in 1853. Most streets have been named to honor the early settlers of the area. However, by taking any of the streets heading south from Main Street toward the beach, the visitor travels fast forward in architectural time to the latter part of the twentieth century. Here, the wetlands have become the setting for much experimentation in modern architectural forms. Many styles – some clever, some attractive, some grotesque, but all exclusive – are represented here, and the view across Moriches Bay reveals the outlines of still further architectural innovations along Dune Road.

The entire western section of Southampton Township was purchased from the Indians in the early 1600s. One of the first settlements here was known as Beaver Dam and was located at what is now the intersection of Montauk Highway (Route 27), Mill Road, and Old Country Road. In Colonial times it was the site of the area's first mill, church, and meetinghouse and it became the hub

A late summer thunderstorm menaces East Hampton.

of activity for the Western Hamptons. Montauk Highway and the Long Island Railroad, which run roughly parallel to each other all the way to Montauk Point, are the boundaries of a geographical feature that has determined the character of the area. Land to the south of the railroad is more fertile, and subsequently most of the larger homes and estates are located in this region. To the north of the railroad, the land is flat, the soil sandy, and the only supportable foliage is scrub oak and scrub pine. This flat land, with its easy access to New York City, has made twentieth-century Long Island an ideal spot for airports. In fact, to the north of Westhampton is Suffolk County Airport, a multi-use site which provides facilities for executive jets, sightseeing charters, and air taxis from Manhattan. But its most visible portion is that used by the military, or the New York Air National Guard, for the airport is the home of the 106th Aerospace Reserve and Recovery Group, which provides support for Coast Guard rescue operations in the area.

Just south of Montauk Highway is the village of Westhampton Beach. Stylish clothing shops, antique stores, restaurants and boutiques occupy the heart of this village. In addition, real estate offices are everywhere since buying, selling, renting or leasing houses is big business. Although quiet in the winter, once the season begins Westhampton Beach is buzzing with shoppers, weekend visitors, and summer guests busy seeing and being seen. Some of the most beautiful homes in the Hamptons are located on the outskirts of Westhampton Beach, where three centuries of architectural

The bays and inlets of the Hamptons provide a tranquil setting for the area's beautiful homes.

Potatoes – the basic crop of Long Island farmers for over a century.

styles are represented. That's no surprise given that the entire Westhampton Beach region was acquired in 1666 from the Indians on terms established in the "Quogue Purchase." The land was used for sheep and cattle grazing until the early eighteenth century, when settlements were gradually established. It wasn't until the middle of the nineteenth century that the area was "discovered" as a summer vacation haven. The Long Island Railroad, which went straight to Speonk, facilitated travel to the area and boarding houses soon sprang up in Westhampton Beach. In 1866, Howell House opened for business as the area's first summer hotel, helping to establish the tourist business that is so successful today.

The houses built between the village of Westhampton Beach and the ocean are for the most part in the classic Hampton style of shingled houses with well-kept lawns and high privet

hedges. But this changes as we cross the drawbridge that takes us to the barrier island and its main thoroughfare, Dune Road. This barrier island runs parallel to the South Fork from the Moriches inlet south of Remsenburg all the way to Southampton, interrupted only by the Shinnecock inlet. The island is quite narrow, in some places less than a hundred yards wide, and features an almost continuous ridge of high sand dunes. Driving along Dune Road one catches only occasional glimpses of the Atlantic: the ocean views are obscured either by the dunes or, more often, by the houses. Most of this property is private and a public beach is a rare find. The houses along Dune Road are quite close together because ocean-front land is at a premium. Most of the houses are designed with panels of glass or large windows to make the most of the views. Constructed primarily of wood shingles and siding,

Winter's traces are visible on this Sagaponack farm.

often sprouting circular towers, staircases, archways and cantilevered balconies, these homes run the gamut from the stylish and elegant to the gaudy and banal. What they all share, despite their individual architectural eccentricities, is the sensation of being precariously perched on a narrow strip of land that is subject to the violence of the storms and hurricanes that often roll in off the Atlantic. For this reason the houses are generally built on stilts or wooden pilings that have been driven into the dunes in order to lend some stability to their structure. Attempts have been made in the past to reinforce the dunes; nonetheless, insurance companies, recognizing the power of the Atlantic, are reluctant to grant insurance policies to local homeowners.

Across Aspatuck Creek to the east of Westhampton are the villages of Quogue and Quiogue. Quogue first appears on the Southampton Town Record in 1651, when rights were sold for cutting salt hay to feed cattle in winter. The etymology of the name Quogue is in dispute. It is thought to be a shortened version of Quaquanantuck, which in the local Indian language meant: "a cove or estuary where the land quakes or trembles" – a fitting name for marshlands growing salt hay. Since it is located on the ocean, Quogue also supported a thriving business selling products obtained from beached and stranded whales. At that time, whales were plentiful enough to make such trade profitable – in fact, records from the late 1600s show that hundreds of barrels of whale oil were sold annually in this region.

Several landmarks survive from

East Hampton barns, bathed in the purple glow of a winter twilight.

these earlier times. A visit to the old Quogue cemetery reveals tombstones bearing the names of the village forefathers. The family names of Cook, Foster and Rogers belong to the first permanent settlers who came to this area from Southampton. Another landmark, a two-room schoolhouse built in 1822, now houses the local museum. The Quogue library, opened in 1897, and the Quogue Community Hall are still pivotal in the life of the community. Religion also played a prominent role in nineteenth-century lives and Quogue has some fine examples of places of worship. The Presbyterian Church and the Episcopal Church of the Atonement are particularly noteworthy not only for their unique, shingle-style architecture, but also because they reflect the importance of religion in early Long Island history. In the late 1800s, the railroad brought the summer crowd to Quogue, marking the advent of the boarding-house era, which declined again after World War I, to be replaced by the building of large, private summer homes.

Despite development in the area, fauna can still be viewed in a natural setting at the Quogue Wildlife Refuge, located near Montauk Highway and run by the New York State Conservation Department. The refuge provides a sanctuary for animals that have been found hurt or wounded, and local wildlife can be viewed along its nature trails.

Hampton Bays lies just east of Quogue. What makes this town unique is its geography – here, the gentle hills of the South Fork level out and the land practically disappears at Canoe Place, a name that harks back to the days of the Shinnecock Indians when the area was the site of a canoe portage.

The stark silhouettes of modernistic buildings cannot compete with the drama of a fiery sunset along Dune Road, Southampton.

The lighthouse at Montauk: Long Island's signature monument.

Canoe Place is a narrow isthmus that separates Great Peconic Bay to the north from Shinnecock Bay to the south. In all likelihood it was the Indians who created the first canal by excavating, or perhaps expanding, a small stream connecting the bays. Approximately three quarters of a mile long, the canal is equipped with tidal gates to control the flow of water and a lock to allow boats to pass through the canal. Finally, in 1892, the canal was opened and boats could travel freely between the bays. Shinnecock Bay was separated from the Atlantic by the strip of barrier island to its south until the hurricane of 1938 burst through the beach front there and allowed the Atlantic to surge in, forming the Shinnecock Inlet. The area's inhabitants were pleased with their new access to the Atlantic, and made this passage permanent in 1956 by constructing rock jetties off the mouth of the inlet. From that time on, boats have sailed back and forth from Great Peconic Bay between the forks to Moriches Bay and out to the Atlantic Ocean. It was the combination of bays, land, and inlets that made Hampton Bays a hub for commercial and recreational fishing, as well as for pleasure boating of all kinds.

Canoe Place Inn, the original of which was built in 1750 by Jeremiah Culver, stakes a claim to being the first building in the Hampton Bays area. What began as a small house for Culver, eventually became first a stagecoach stop and then, with further additions over the years, an inn. This site has hosted many important regional events. In 1892, John L. Sullivan trained for the upcoming defense of his heavyweight championship title against James Corbett in the barn located behind the

The ocean rolls toward the shore at Montauk.

Time has textured the tombstones of the graves of East Hampton's founders.

inn. In the early 1900s, Ernest Buchmuller, formerly of Manhattan's Waldorf Astoria, purchased the inn; following his death, his stepson sold it in 1917 to Julius Keller, who owned the well-known Manhattan restaurant, Maxim's. Although a fire destroyed the inn in 1921, Keller rebuilt it and even added on cottages. For over thirty years, one of these cottages was the summer home of Alfred E. Smith, governor of New York State. Indeed, the area has always been a magnet for politicians. Judge Wauhope Lynn, once a state Senator, built a large estate on Shinnecock Bay in the late 1800s, and encouraged other politicians, such as S. R. Croker and Charles F. Murphy,

both heads of New York City's Tammany Hall political organization, to come to the area, where they then built palatial homes.

Yet another attraction of the Canoe Place area was the Shinnecock Casino. Wealthy Hampton dwellers came to try their luck in the casino, and its popularity did not falter despite fear of police raids. In the early part of this century, the casino burned down three or four times, always under mysterious circumstances. The story goes that these fires always preceded the rumor of a raid. During Prohibition, the Canoe Place area was again raided by the police because of both the many illegally operated stills and the rum-

running activities in the bay region.

Near to Canoe Place is Squiretown. Historically important as an early settlement where, in 1773, Ellis Squire and his wife, Phoebe, built a cabin on what is now known as Squire's pond, the area is today completely residential. The house built in 1783 by their son Ellis Squire Jr. is still standing at the intersection of Squiretown and Newtown Roads. Another family member, Seth, built a home in the Squiretown area in 1786, and this, too, remains. However, the Squires weren't the only family from this period whose houses still stand – the home of the Fournier family, whose members served in the American Revolution,

also remains.

Just south of Hampton Bays is an historic section called Punquogue. The Joseph Penny family settled this area on Shinnecock Bay. Meanwhile, Punquogue was where Judge Lynn owned large tracts of land, and the major road there, Lynn Avenue, still bears his name. As with all of the South Fork, access to the Atlantic Ocean beaches of the barrier island is of prime importance. Punquogue boasts a modern bridge that carries motorists to public beaches and parks. The area's beaches, plus its boating facilities, which boast direct access to the bays and to the ocean, make Hampton Bays a prime recreational region.

White wooden shingles – covering churches or residences – represent the preferred architectural style of the Hamptons in the nineteenth and early twentieth century.

CENTRAL HAMPTONS

Heading eastward on Montauk Highway from Canoe Place across the Shinnecock Canal, we come to the section called Shinnecock Hills. Here, the road hugs the shore of Shinnecock Bay and affords a pleasant view. The Shinnecock Hills themselves are large sand dunes covered with scrub pine and beach grass, and are reminiscent of the Scottish moors. This likeness is reflected in local place names, such as the landmark Scotch Mist Inn. Dr. A. H. Ely of New York City, President Warren Harding's personal physician, built this mansion in 1918 as his residence. Harding not only visited Ely at his home, built on twenty-six acres of Shinnecock Hills land, but made one of the wings his summer White House. The entire house consisted of thirty rooms, most with magnificent views of both the Great Peconic and Shinnecock bays as well as of the Atlantic Ocean, and it was designed by the architect Grosvenor Attenbury. In 1949, the house and land were purchased by Mathias Wayne and served guests as the Scotch Mist Inn until 1968, when the building was entirely destroyed by fire.

On the eastern section of the Shinnecock Hills stands Southampton College, a branch of Long Island University. The campus is the current home of an historic windmill, which dates back to 1712 and was moved here from the village of Southampton. What is now the college was once the Arthur B. Clafflin estate known as Heathermere. Built in 1898, the estate house had thirty rooms, and Clafflin furnished it by purchasing the entire contents of a European castle, which were then shipped to Southampton. In 1963 the estate became a college, and

An East Hampton mansion looks across the dunes to the Atlantic Ocean.

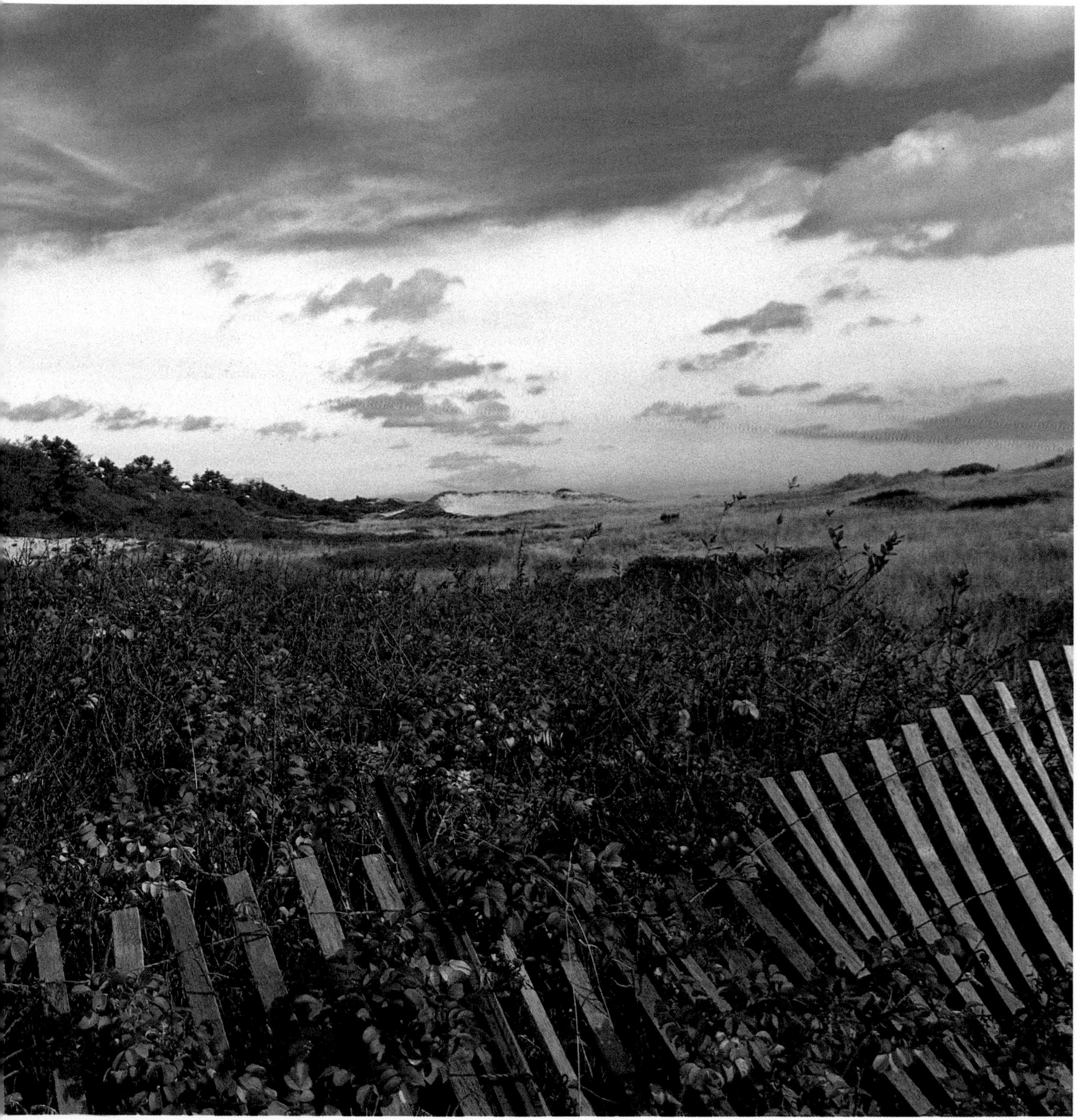

in 1983 it merged with C. W. Post College in Brookville, Long Island.

At the eastern end of Shinnecock Bay is a large neck of land which has been set aside as the Shinnecock Indian Reservation. This is the oldest Native American reservation in the United States. Deeds record that it was established in 1701, and New York State confirmed the Shinnecock Indian's right to the land by giving them title to the area known as Shinnecock Neck in 1859. The name, Shinnecock, means "the good ground," and these Indians are just one of the thirteen Long Island tribes that made up the Montauk Confederacy, the others being the Canarsie, Rockaway, Matinecock, Merrick, Massapequa, Secatogue, Setauket, Nissaquogue, Unkechaug, Shinnecock, Montaukett, Corchaug, and Manhasset tribes. The Shinnecock Indians occupy the same territory on which they were found by settlers in 1640; this represents a departure from the general practice of herding Indians onto lands other than their native ones. Each year in early September, the Shinnecock Indians hold a powwow to which all are invited to observe their culture and customs.

The Shinnecock Indians lived in dome-shaped wigwams made from saplings and rushes, and they were hunters and herdsmen as well as farmers. Like many Long Islanders, they also sustained themselves by fishing in the bays and seas that surrounded them. The Shinnecock tribe welcomed the arrival of white settlers in 1640, not only giving them land to live on, but also sharing with the settlers their knowledge of fishing and harvesting the clams and scallops from nearby bays. Without the help of

Pheasants, though not native to America, have proliferated on Long Island's East End.

Sag Harbor homes are a constant reminder of the glory days of the whaling industry. Lovingly preserved behind its white picket fence, this house seems to invite the onlooker into another world.

these Indians, it is believed that the early settlers would most likely not have survived. The relationship between local Indians and white settlers was friendlier than in other parts of the country, and the Shinnecock Indians continue to exist amicably with the community.

In June of 1640, a group of English settlers traveling from New England in small boats crossed Great Peconic Bay, entered the harbor now known as North Sea, and landed at Conscience Point, which could be considered the Plymouth Rock of the South Fork. The parallel between the two landings is underscored by the Southampton Colonial Society's having placed at

the spot where the settlers disembarked a plaque on a boulder with the inscription: "Near this spot in June, 1640, landed colonists from Lynn, Mass. who founded Southampton, the first English settlement in New York State." The Indians gave the settlers a section of land now known as "Olde Towne" in the village of Southampton. The original deed from the Indians, dated 1640, has survived to this day, and is kept at the Town Hall along with other historical documents of the Colonial period. This settlement was called Southampton after the British Earl of Southampton, and from here settlers spread throughout the South Fork, carrying the Hampton part of the name with them.

Development in this area was slow. The settlers considered themselves fortunate because nature had been so kind to the area – the climate was tempered by the ocean, keeping the winters mild and the summers cool. The village of Southampton still features fine examples of architecture from this founding period. The Thomas Halsey Homestead, also known as "Hollyhocks," was built in the late 1640s, and is reputed to be the oldest frame house still standing in New York State. Another remnant from Colonial times is the old silversmith shop, built in 1686 and located on Main Street. The Rogers Homestead (circa 1840), located on Meetinghouse Lane, now contains the Southampton Historical Museum. Also in the museum grounds is a pre-Revolutionary barn (circa 1740), where British soldiers stabled their horses during the Revolutionary War.

During the eighteenth and nineteenth centuries, fishing and agriculture slowly spread. Located at the easternmost tip of Long Island, the region was isolated from the major battles being fought during the Revolutionary War. Thanks to the remoteness of the region, many landmarks have been preserved and the region has been left virtually untouched by the destruction of early wars.

Large farms in the nineteenth century took to cultivating vegetables, with Long Island potatoes constituting the major crop. As a supplement to vegetable farming, the raising of ducks became an important industry. In fact, it is estimated that approximately half of all the commercially raised ducks in the United States come from Long Island. Local farmers got the idea of importing the Peking breed of ducks

Fall corn decorates the weathered door of the Sag Harbor Express.

from China after a Chinese student, Chan Laisien, gave an address to the Hampton Agricultural Society in 1873, in which he mentioned the great size and quality of the ducks in his homeland. Until that time, ducks in the Hamptons region had been of the European variety, and were characterized by their small size which earned them the nickname "puddle ducks." The region's climate, its sandy soil, and its large number of ponds, inlets and bays created a natural environment for the duck industry. However, without access to the great consumer market of New York City, the industry would always have remained in its infancy. Indeed, it did not hit the big time until the Long Island Railroad extended affordable transportation to Eastport in 1868.

The duck industry was not all that the arrival of the railroad changed. When the railroad extended its operations eastward to Sag Harbor in 1872, making the area readily accessible to wealthy New Yorkers seeking respite from the rapidly growing city, the concept of the Hamptons as an escape from urban pressures was born. New Yorkers of substance and wealth caused a building boom at the eastern end of Long Island. Large estates were designed and built and the village of Southampton grew and prospered as it catered to the whims and demands of "the summer crowd." One landmark of this era is The Orchard, a mansion built in 1905 for J. L. Breese, a broker and engineer. This building, which stands on Hill Street, was designed by Stanford White; in 1926, it was sold to Charles E. Merrill of the Wall Street firm of Merrill, Lynch. The local landmark preservation society

The interplay of light and moisture bring a touch of magic to the charm of the Hamptons.

campaigned to have the building declared an historic site. Other buildings from this period were less fortunate. The Hampton Manor, a hotel built around 1880, suffered the all-too-common fate of being torn down to make way for a shopping center in the mid-1950s.

The increasing wealth of the region during the late nineteenth and early twentieth centuries was reflected in the growth of private organizations and clubs. The Meadow Club, founded in 1883, and the Shinnecock Golf Club, founded in 1891, are reputed to be among the oldest country clubs in the United States, while the Southampton Riding and Hunt Club and the Southampton Yacht Club are later examples of what represents a trend toward exclusivity.

Toward the end of the nineteenth century, the arts began to flourish in the Hamptons. One of the earliest patrons of the arts from this region, Samuel L. Parrish, donated the land for an art school to be built in Southampton in 1897, a project which was then realized by Mrs. William Hoyt of Shinnecock Hills. She arranged for the artist William Merritt Chase to serve as instructor for the school, which was modeled after the Barbizon School in France. Known as the Art Village, the school operated between 1891 and 1902. This was not Parrish's only contribution to the arts. In 1897, he acquired land in Southampton Village adjacent to the Rogers-Memorial Library, and commissioned Grosvenor Attenbury to build a museum large enough to house his extensive art collection. Over the years the museum has expanded, and it is still a major cultural center today. The area owes

Grasses provide protection for the fragile ecology of the dunes.

41

Hamptons style – Junior Division.

other historic landmarks to Grosvenor Attenbury, a prominent local architect and town planner, who apprenticed under Stanford White, and designed several of the area's homes and churches. Attenbury is, however, perhaps best known as the architect of the American Wing of the Metropolitan Museum of Art in New York City. The Hamptons have served as both setting and inspiration for many of the region's artists. In particular, Fairfield Porter lived in Southampton and his works are frequently exhibited at the Parrish Art Museum.

The car emerged as the most popular form of transportation for Hampton visitors in the early twentieth century. This is still the case, something vividly attested to by the weekend traffic jams in the Hamptons. But the car is by no means the only mode of transportation. Some visitors still use the Long Island Railroad, some come by private jet or helicopter, and others use a motor coach service called the Hampton Jitney. First run in the mid-1970s to bring bicyclists to the Hamptons during the oil crisis, the Hampton Jitney has claimed a place as one of the more stylish ways of travelling from Manhattan to the Hamptons. It features quality club-class service on a coach painted in a distinctive wave-like design created by famed Pop artist Roy Lichtenstein.

The young set inherits the traditions of The Maidstone Club.

The greater Southampton area includes the towns of North Sea and Noyack on the Great Peconic Bay side of Southampton. Noyack boasts the Morton National Wildlife refuge, located on Jessup's Neck, where it is possible to view the landscape in its natural state, and even to glimpse the occasional deer.

Watermill, Bridgehampton, Mecox, Sagaponack, and Wainscott are all small towns to the east of Southampton. Watermill is one of the oldest towns on Long Island, having been founded in 1644 when the town of Southampton gave Edward Howell forty acres of land on the condition that he "build for himself to supply the necessities of the towne, a sufficient mill at Mecoxe." The mill Howell built no longer stands, although another mill, built in 1800 and moved in 1814, still marks the spot he originally selected, and is now a museum.

The name Bridgehampton reflects the town's history inasmuch as it was the site of a bridge across Sogg Pond, which once separated Mecox from Sagaponack. Today, Bridgehampton is a much larger town than either of those the bridge originally connected. Bridgehampton is characterized by beautiful homes, old churches and historic windmills; one windmill in particular – the Berwind Mill – was built in Sag Harbor in 1820 and moved to Bridgehampton in 1837. It is well maintained and located on a picturesque spot surrounded by attractive formal gardens. Bridge-hampton also hosts several national events, one of the more prominent of which is the Bridgehampton Race Circuit – nationally famous for stock and sport car racing. Meanwhile, the Hampton Classic Horse Show attracts Olympic class horses and riders to compete annually for prestigious prizes, and the Bridgehampton winery grows grapes and produces wines of a very high caliber, for which it has won awards in state competitions. The winery can be visited for both information and tastings.

Sagaponack is a very small town with a very long history, attested to by the old tombstones in the Sogg Common cemetery. Some of the architectural gems here include an old saltbox-style home dating back to around 1700, an old schoolhouse and a quaint general store still in operation. Today, Sagaponack is also a showplace of modern architecture and boasts award-winning homes, each of unique design, and all gracing what was once farmland.

SAG HARBOR

Sag Harbor, differing in appearance and character from Southampton, is another major attraction in the Central Hampton area. Located on the bay side of the South Fork, Sag Harbor offered a better and safer harbor for ships than did the coast of the Atlantic Ocean. Therefore, in the early 1700s, the inhabitants of Sagg – now called Sagaponack – cut a road through the woods and built a dock for their area at "the harbor of Sagg." The port slowly grew during the eighteenth century as more settlers came from New England. A reminder of this period still stands today – the Old Custom House, built around 1789. Not only was it the first Custom House in all of New York State,

A pattern of picket fences, dappled with fall sunlight, produces a classic Sag Harbor scene.

but it also served as Long Island's first post office.

In the later 1700s, local settlers constructed sailing vessels and ventured forth in search of whales. The whale-oil business quickly caught on, and the town grew and prospered. In fact, in 1845 there were sixty-three whaling ships and 1,800 men working out of Sag Harbor, not to mention the millions of dollars generated in the area by the sale of whale-related products. At the peak of its prosperity, Sag Harbor rivaled the thriving whaling ports of Salem and New Bedford, Massachusetts. This heritage is preserved in the Whaling Museum on Main Street, which displays whaling ship models, scrimshaw and other artifacts of this period in an historic building, constructed in 1845 by Benjamin Huntting. Minard Lafever, architect for the Whaling Museum, also designed the Old Whaler Presbyterian Church, which was built in 1844. The original church featured a very high steeple, which was designed as a landmark to be sighted by returning sailors; unfortunately, this steeple was another victim of the 1938 hurricane.

This period of prosperity for Sag Harbor ended in 1870 with the demise of the whaling industry; however, this was the same year that the Long Island Railroad pushed its way eastward to the town. Today, Sag Harbor is a boating center with a large marina; a cultural center, home to writers and artists; and a tourist center for people visiting landmarks of the whaling era. Shops and restaurants are yet another of Sag Harbor's attractions, as is the town's access to the ferry to Shelter Island.

Homes were built in the Hamptons by those seeking the peace and tranquility encapsulated in this lilac-tinted scene.

The Eastern Hamptons
East Hampton

Driving east along Montauk Highway through Wainscott, the approach to East Hampton is marked by beautiful homes on either side of this tree-lined road. Just a glimpse of Main Street is enough to convince many why East Hampton has been called "America's Most Beautiful Village." From Main Street one can see Town Pond, which is surrounded by well-manicured grass and has willow trees overhanging its banks. Across the pond is South End Cemetery, which once served as the churchyard of East Hampton's first meetinghouse. Some of the tombstones in this cemetery date back to the seventeenth century, including the tomb of Lion Gardiner, the first white man to settle in the area.

Lion Gardiner was sent to the colonies by the British to build a fort in Connecticut. The fort was supposed to serve the dual purpose of containing both the Dutch and the Indians of the New England area. These Indians, the Pequots and the Narragansetts, were more warlike than the Montauks of eastern Long Island and had, through frequent raids, established the practice of extorting tribute from the Montauks. In 1637, Gardiner and the British attacked the Pequots, breaking their power and establishing an alliance with Wyandanch, the sachem of the Montauks. Thereafter, the Montauks paid tribute to the British, and Gardiner and Wyandanch forged a friendship that was to prove beneficial not only to them, but also to all of the new settlers in the area. Gardiner is remembered for having maintained close relations with the Montauk Indians in the East Hampton-Montauk area. His pact with the Montauks prevented attacks from the Narragansett Indians of New England and kept the peace on the

Sag Harbor celebrates Halloween.

South Fork. While the Montauks' alliance with the British saved them from raids from New England tribes, nothing could protect them from the ravages of smallpox and measles. As they became assimilated into the culture of the colonists, the Montauks' language and many of their customs

The classic lines of this Sag Harbor church stand out crisp and clear in the fall air.

died out. The Indians were also prone to alcoholism, and fell victim to unprincipled white settlers who manipulated them by supplying them with rum. Lyman Beecher, an East Hampton minister and father of Harriet Beecher Stowe, railed against these practices, but it was a losing battle. By the mid-nineteenth century there were only a handful of Montauk Indian families left.

It was from Wyandanch that Gardiner purchased the island that still bears his name. King Charles I granted Gardiner this land in 1639, and it has been in the possession of the Gardiner family ever since. Gardiners Island, six miles long and three miles wide, is located in Napeague Bay approximately three miles from the mainland of East Hampton. For the last 300 years Gardiner and his descendants have maintained possession of the tiny island, and their history has not been uneventful. Lion Gardiner's daughter, Elizabeth, fell ill and in the throes of a fever accused one of the local women of witchcraft. As a result of Elizabeth's accusation, the woman, Goodwife Garlick, was sent back to the Connecticut Colony to be tried as a witch. Ultimately, she was released on the condition that her husband, Joshua Garlick, pay a fine of thirty pounds sterling.

Even more dramatic than a witch-hunt was the arrival on Gardiners Island of the notorious pirate Captain Kidd. Kidd paid a visit to John Gardiner, grandson of Lion Gardiner, and entrusted him with his treasure. Kidd and his men buried an assortment of gold, silver and precious stones in a swamp on the island, and some believe that the bulk of the treasure is still there today. In 1765, John Gardiner's great-grandson David inherited the island and built an elegant new manor

house there, which stood until 1947 when it was destroyed by fire. The Gardiner family name gained national prominence with Julia Gardiner, another of Lion's descendants, who married President John Tyler and became well known as a fashionable First Lady and hostess in Washington, D.C.

Although Gardiners Island is inaccessible to the public, the village of East Hampton preserves enough history of its own to satisfy most visitors. Adjacent to the South End Cemetery and village green is the seventeenth-century saltbox-style house known as "Home Sweet Home." Owned by John Howard Payne, composer of the famous song of that name, Home Sweet Home is beautifully preserved and open to the public. Another mid-seventeenth-century building, the Mulford House, was owned by the family of that name until 1948 and now serves as the home of the East Hampton Historical Society.

In a pattern that recurred throughout the South Fork, the latter part of the nineteenth century marked the arrival in the area of wealthy New Yorkers, who came to Long Island to build homes and estates. These newcomers gravitated toward East Hampton, as it was still beyond the reach of the railroad and was consequently more exclusive than neighboring towns. Attracted by the beauty of the area, artists such as Winslow Homer and Childe Hassam also flocked to East Hampton during the 1870s, contributing to the town's prestige as an artists' colony. In this century, giants such as Salvador Dali, Marcel Duchamp and Fernand Léger added their names to the list of artists

Fences help stabilize the shifting beach sands, blown by the wintery winds that have also carved the snow into "waves."

who sought out the peace and beauty of the Hamptons.

In present-day East Hampton, Guild Hall and the John Drew Theater are the nucleus of the area's cultural life. The John Drew Theater was named after the turn-of-the-century actor John Drew, who lived in East Hampton, where he frequently entertained his niece Ethel Barrymore. In addition to being an important celebrity, Drew was an integral part of the social whirl of the Maidstone Club. The Maidstone was the precursor of the many exclusive clubs which were established to protect the privacy of the wealthy and to provide recreation for those who enjoyed tennis, golf, the breeding of horses and the occasional fox hunt.

Today, visitors are attracted to the antique shops, galleries, bookstores and upscale boutiques and restaurants of modern-day East Hampton. Beautiful homes and estates encircle the village, and are set amongst the ponds and inlets that dot this region. At the east end of East Hampton, the traveller notices Hook Mill, an historic windmill, built in 1866 and still in good working order. The mill is open to visitors and is of particular interest because of its authentic wooden machinery.

The next stop east is Amagansett, a town whose Indian name literally means "place of good water." Indians and early settlers came to Amagansett to draw fresh water from the town's wells, the location of which is commemorated today by a boulder and a plaque. In the nineteenth century, Amagansett was home to whaling and fishing captains and their crews, a

From commercial fishing boats to luxurious yachts, the marina provides a safe harbor for all craft.

tradition that is preserved in the Marine Museum of the town. The sea has always been a source of both income and surprise to inhabitants of the region. An important part of the early Amagansett economy was disposing of beached whales and selling whale oil at considerable profit. Wreckage from all over the North Atlantic has been known to wash up on these shores. One of the sea's most unpleasant surprises, however, came during World War II when four German saboteurs were dropped on the beach by an offshore submarine. These Germans were later apprehended heading for New York City, and were executed before they could do any damage. Just the same, the incident vividly brought home to Long Islanders the realities of war. Today, the descendants of earlier Amagansett dwellers play host to the summer visitors who come to enjoy the magnificent stretches of white sandy beaches and to view the picturesque town.

To the east of Amagansett, the geography takes a dramatic turn as the land narrows to the slender strip leading up to Montauk Point. With the Atlantic on one side and Napeague Bay on the other, the region is sometimes hilly and is characterized by sand dunes and a constant sea breeze of clean ocean air. Parts of Napeague are so barren that they seem like a moonscape – the rolling dunes are covered by low grasses and green-gray moss. Naturalists not only seek out the unusual plant life here, but are equally intrigued by the rare birds that have been sighted. Observing ospreys that patrol the skies searching for food for

Mansions built among the dunes bravely face the Atlantic.

A windmill in Sag Harbor serves both as a reminder of life in earlier times and as an information center in today's world.

themselves and their young is another opportunity Napeague affords.

One other thing that sets this area apart from the rest of the Hamptons is the so-called "walking dunes" – the sands comprising these dunes shift, moving according to the pressures of natural forces such as wind and water. The dunes and salt meadows still appear much as they did in earlier times, and vegetation such as beach plums and grasses, on which cattle

and livestock graze, abound. This area was the home of the Montaukett Indians, a tribe dating back at least 4,000 years. The name Montauk means "hilly country," and these Indians tended herds of sheep and cattle as well as hunting and fishing in order to survive. When the white settlers arrived, they continued the practice of grazing sheep and cattle here. These early ranchers laid out the Old Montauk Highway in the 1700s in order to market their cattle.

At the same time, Montauk, with its unique location at the eastern tip of Long Island, was the object of several entrepreneurial projects. Developers such as Arthur Benson, Austin Corbin

and Carl Fisher took turns attempting to realize their dreams of turning Montauk into either a prime, deep-water port for ships from Europe or a world-class resort.

In 1879 Arthur Benson bought the entire region now known as Montauk in order to build homes and create a resort. He had a strong track record as a developer; in fact, his success in Brooklyn is still attested to by the Bensonhurst neighborhood, which bears his name. In order to make Montauk a first-class development, Benson hired Frederick Law Olmstead, the landscape architect best known for designing Central Park and Prospect Park to lay out the grounds of his new

Windmills from simple to elaborate were once a major feature of the Long Island landscape. Now most windmills are found only on the East End and are merely decorative.

project, and he engaged the firm of McKim, Mead and White to build homes there. Several of these homes can still be seen today.

In 1895, Austin Corbin, then president of the Long Island Rail Road Company, made the decision to extend the tracks to Montauk, and to do so he bought up thousands of acres of land there. Corbin believed that if Montauk became a major port, the railroad would afford handy access to New York City.

Another developer offering an even more ambitious vision of the future of Montauk was Carl Fisher, builder of the Indianapolis Speedway and a developer of Miami Beach. He headed to Montauk in order to make his fortune. First, he built an office tower for himself, and then he built Montauk Manor – a golf course, beach and yacht club. He also opened the jetty into Lake Montauk, thereby changing the lake from fresh to salt water. Although his plans may have been sound, his timing was off; the Great Depression shattered his dreams. In 1931, Fisher declared bankruptcy, and a few years later he died of alcoholism.

Besides Fisher's Tower, there are only a handful of buildings remaining from the early days of Montauk. The Second House Museum is the oldest surviving building, and is now a museum. Built in the mid-1700s, it was the residence of the area's cattle and sheep herders. Another early building, Third House, is the present-day headquarters of Hither Hills State Park, but was once known as Camp Wyckoff and served as Theodore Roosevelt's headquarters in 1898. Teddy and his Rough Riders, a band of approximately 25,000 men, returned to this site in order to recuperate from the effects of yellow fever contracted during the

Spanish-American War.

Today, Montauk is perhaps best known for sports fishing, and the town boasts more fishing records and trophies than any other port in the world. Charter boats, party boats, and boats that visitors can captain themselves are all available to fishermen who want to try their luck at catching blue-fin tuna, swordfish, marlin, striped bass, mako sharks, and flounders. Naturally, there are a number of excellent seafood restaurants in Montauk, serving those visitors who don't fancy catching and cleaning their own dinners. There are also beaches, harbors and lakes among the dunes and hills of this region, as well as several large state parks for camping, hiking and boating.

Finally, the South Fork comes to an end at Montauk Point. The lighthouse here is the most famous landmark on Long Island. Built in 1797 by order of President George Washington, the sandstone lighthouse tower supports a lantern that is visible from twenty-five miles out to sea. Now 125 miles east of New York City, we have come as far as we can on Long Island, but can look forward to revisiting and exploring the regions of the South Fork. For, as T. S. Eliot wrote:

"We shall not cease from exploration
And the end of all our exploring
Will be to arrive where we started
And know the place for the first time."

The green farms of Sagaponack.

The white-painted wood of the Presbyterian Church stands out against the blue of the East Hampton sky.

The charm of East Hampton is also preserved in its historic cemeteries.

All of Long Island is a haven for migrating waterfowl. Overleaf: Canadian geese take a rest at a peaceful farm near Bridgehampton.

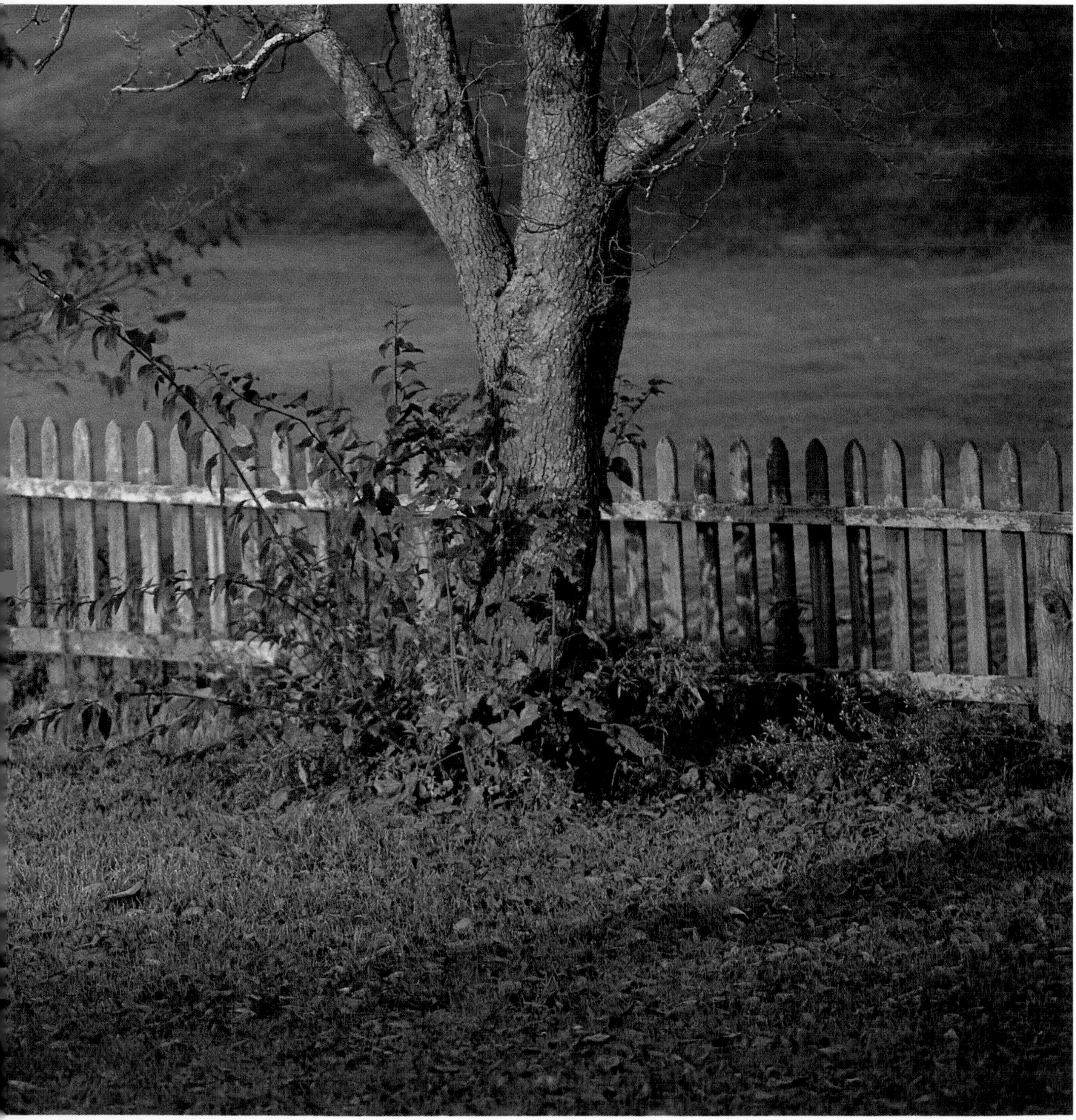

The freshness of springtime – dewdrops cling to delicate white iris flowers.

The pleasure of walking the tree-shaded lanes of East Hampton.

Fishing on the East End provides not only recreation for visitors but also a livelihood for the commercial fishermen who work Peconic Bay and the Atlantic Ocean off Montauk Point.

Beautiful girls – a feature of the Hamptons at any age.

The golf courses of the South Fork have hosted some prestigious tournaments, but amateurs also enjoy the challenge.

The fading light of day gives a rich color to this East Hampton barn, burnishing its windows to copper.

The Whaling Museum at Sag Harbor preserves the artifacts of the town's years as a whaling center, when it rivaled those of Salem and New Bedford in Massachusetts.

Local happenings are always of interest to the area's residents.

The waterfront of Bulls Head Bay, Southampton, provides a peaceful setting for a distinctive Hamptons residence.

The ponds and inlets of East Hampton reflect the clouds of a sunny fall day.

A display of Bridgehampton crafts evokes the early rural lifestyle of the area.

Green lawns dotted with clover: a summer retreat for young ladies at Quogue.

Surf casters and strollers enjoy the last moments of sunlight on the beach at East Hampton.

The young of East Hampton occasionally spend an afternoon trying their luck with a fishing pole – and are always happy to have something to show for their perseverance!

Long Island is horse country! People of all ages enjoy horses whether from the sulky, at the Hampton Classic Horse Show, or from the saddle, in the leafy lanes around Southampton.

The Hampton Classic Horse Show at Bridgehampton attracts world-class riders, guaranteeing an exciting competition.

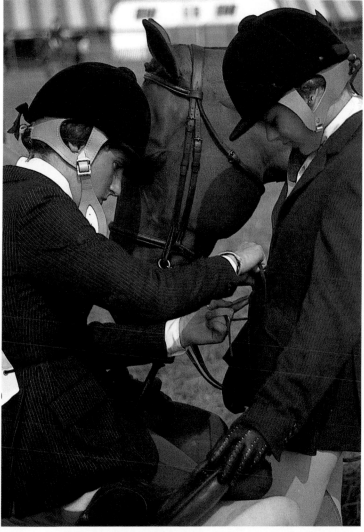

Riders check their own gear as well as the horse's before the competition begins.

The green pastures of a horse farm in Sagaponack.

Canada geese look for a landing spot in the snow to rest awhile on their migratory journey.

Sag Harbor cherishes its heritage and works hard to preserve it – and everyone can appreciate the results.

The garden of John Howard Paine's house, "Home Sweet Home," in East Hampton.

As the Long Island Railroad laid tracks eastward from New York City in the nineteenth century, it brought people and change to the Hamptons.

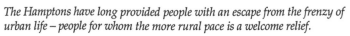

The Hamptons have long provided people with an escape from the frenzy of urban life – people for whom the more rural pace is a welcome relief.

The dying sun illumines the berries of a decorative wreath in Sag Harbor.

Eastern Long Island managed to avoid the physical ravages of wars, thereby preserving many of its oldest buildings. However, there are many reminders of past wars, as this Civil War monument in Sag Harbor attests.

As the chill of a fall evening comes on, a flock of Canada geese prepare for a night in Bridgehampton.

"Season of mists and mellow fruitfulness" ran John Keats' description of fall, a description perfectly fitted to the fields of Bridgehampton.

"If you've got it, flaunt it" – stylish living has been a keystone of life in the Hamptons for over a century.

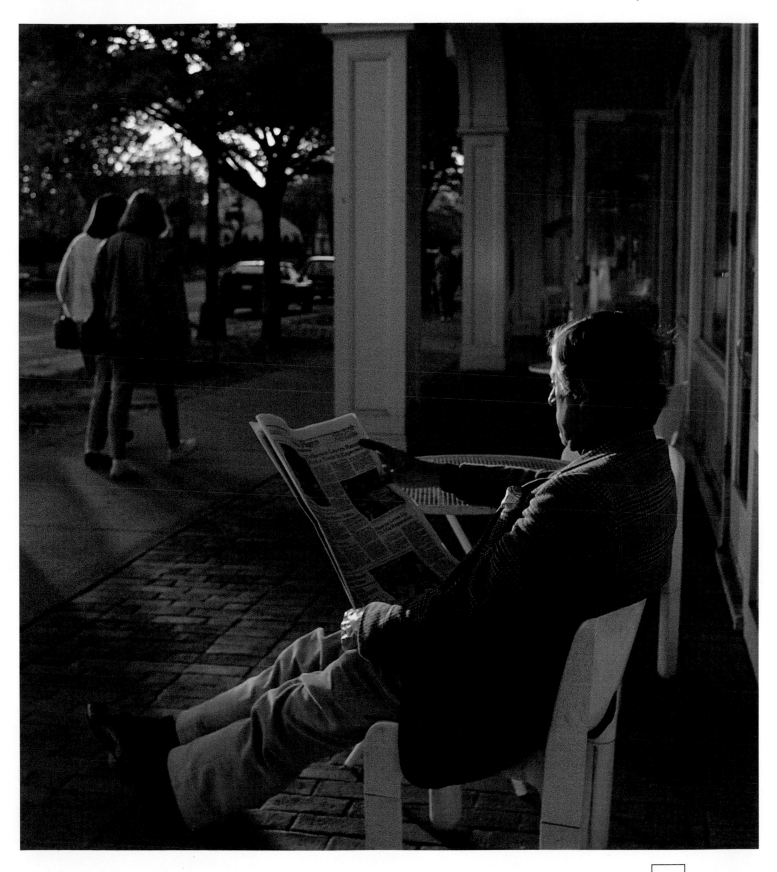

Like pieces in a giant jigsaw puzzle – tidal islands in the flat blue water.

At Sagaponack, and throughout the Hamptons, modern architects employ the shingle patterns of earlier days to unique effect.

Sky and water combine with lush vegetation on the shores of beautiful Hook Pond.

The flat, rich farmlands of Sagaponack, which once produced potatoes by the ton, are slowly giving way to modern mansions – part of the changing face of the Hamptons.

Fall colors and a slanting sun work their magic on the rural scenery of the Hamptons.

Threatened by erosion, the lighthouse at Montauk has nevertheless withstood the batterings of the Atlantic Ocean's waves since the building was commissioned by George Washington in 1797.

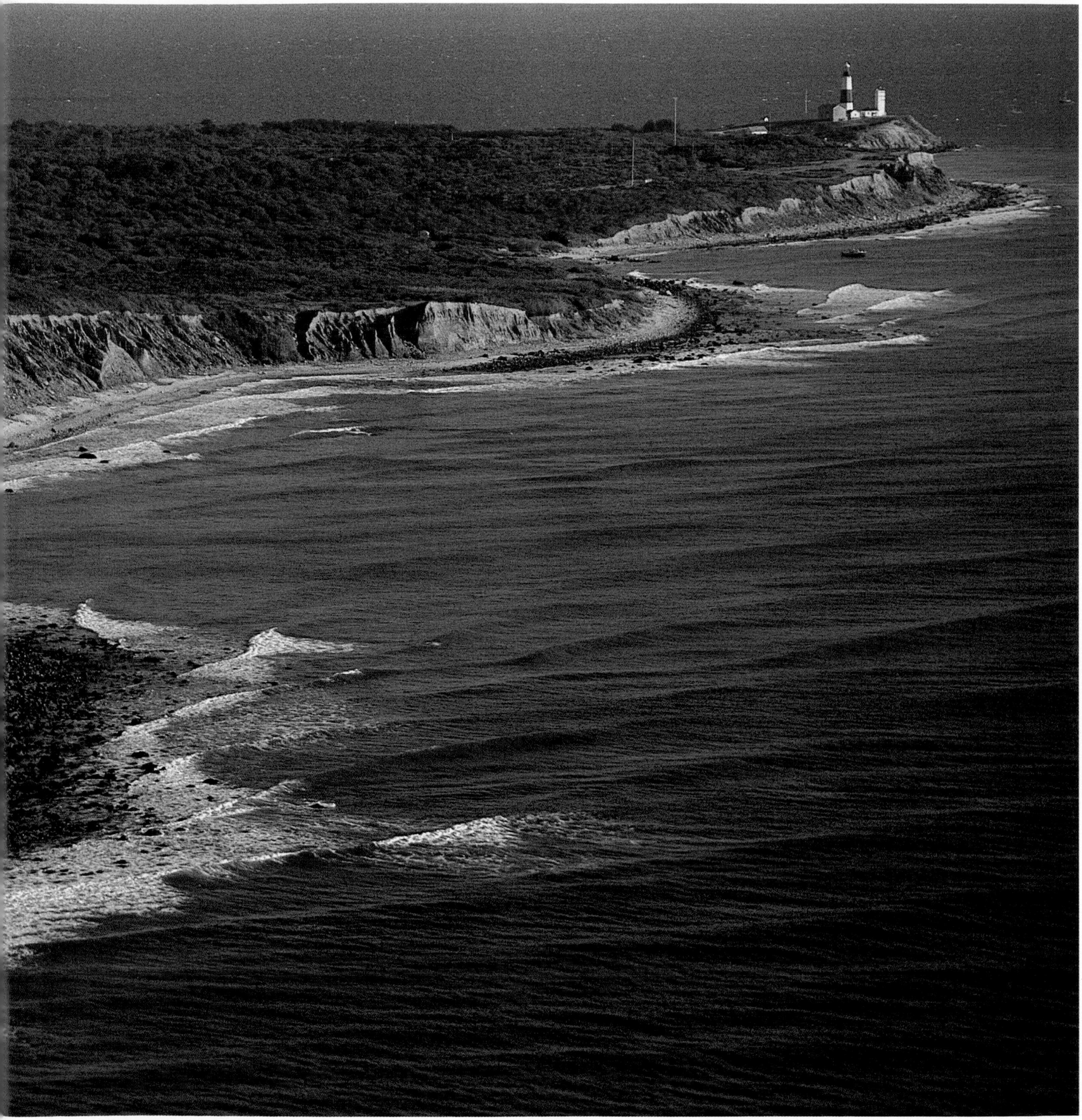

Waves normally roll in peacefully from the Atlantic, but storms and hurricanes can bring sudden changes to the landscape.

The Maidstone Club preserves a century of exclusive privilege in East Hampton.

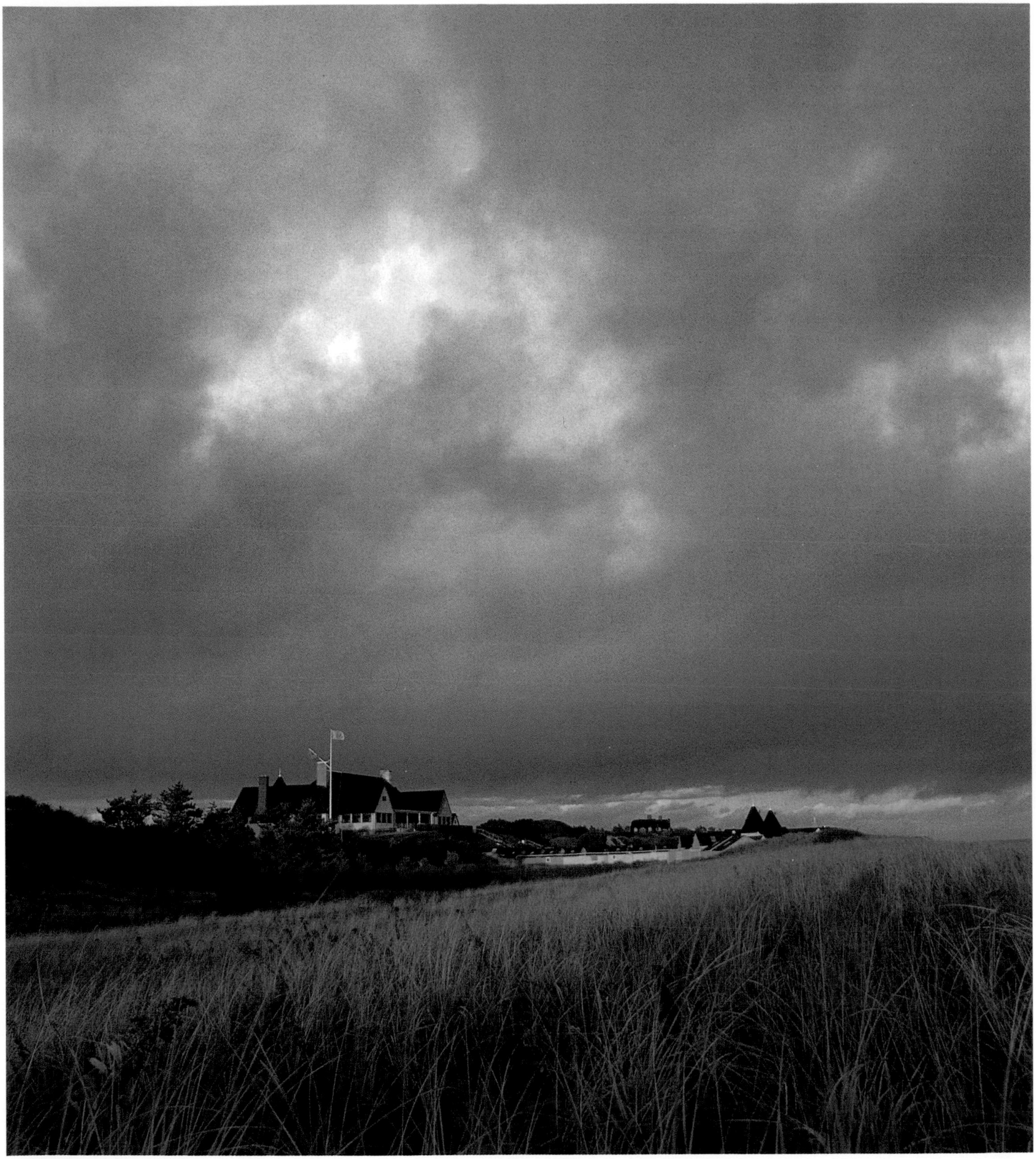

Some of the attractions of the Hamptons – the ocean beaches, ponds and fertile soil of Sagaponack.

The sandy soil of Montauk forms fragile cliffs – the handiwork of the Atlantic Ocean.

A dramatic sweep of ocean beach – as the rising sun gilds the spray blown back from the waves.

A Sag Harbor landmark building flies the flag.

Trees and shrubs furnish borders to the marsh and farmland at North Sea, near Southampton.

As the fall sun sets, long shadows reach across this East Hampton field.